# THE GREAT
# ARTISTS

## Paul Cezanne

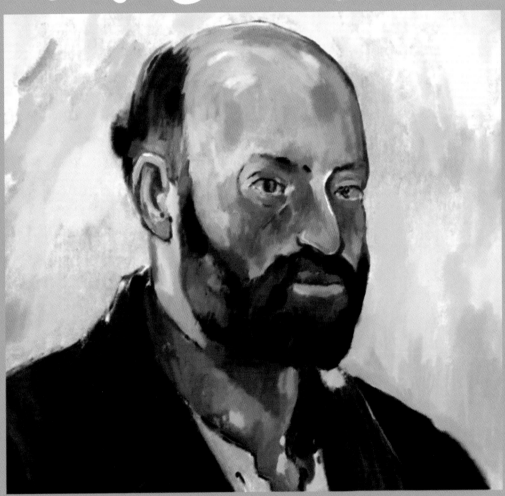

### Anjali Raghbeer

An imprint of Om Books International

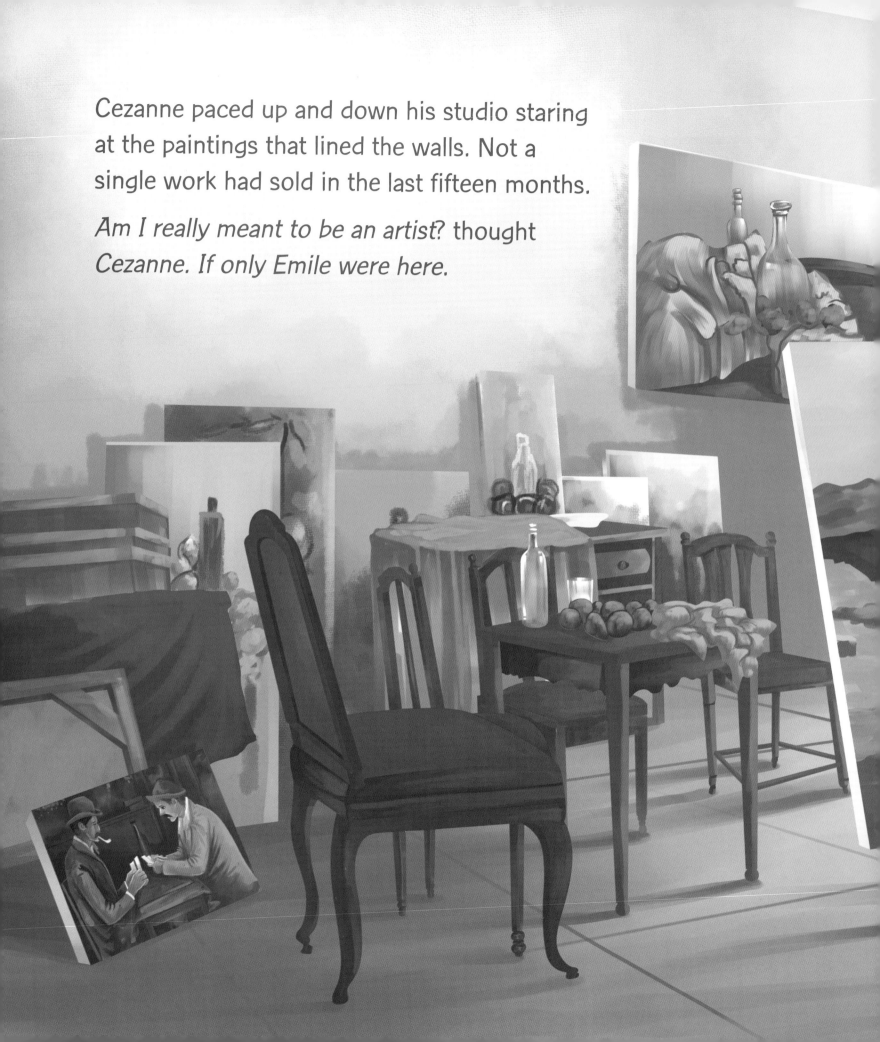

Cezanne paced up and down his studio staring at the paintings that lined the walls. Not a single work had sold in the last fifteen months.

*Am I really meant to be an artist?* thought Cezanne. *If only Emile were here.*

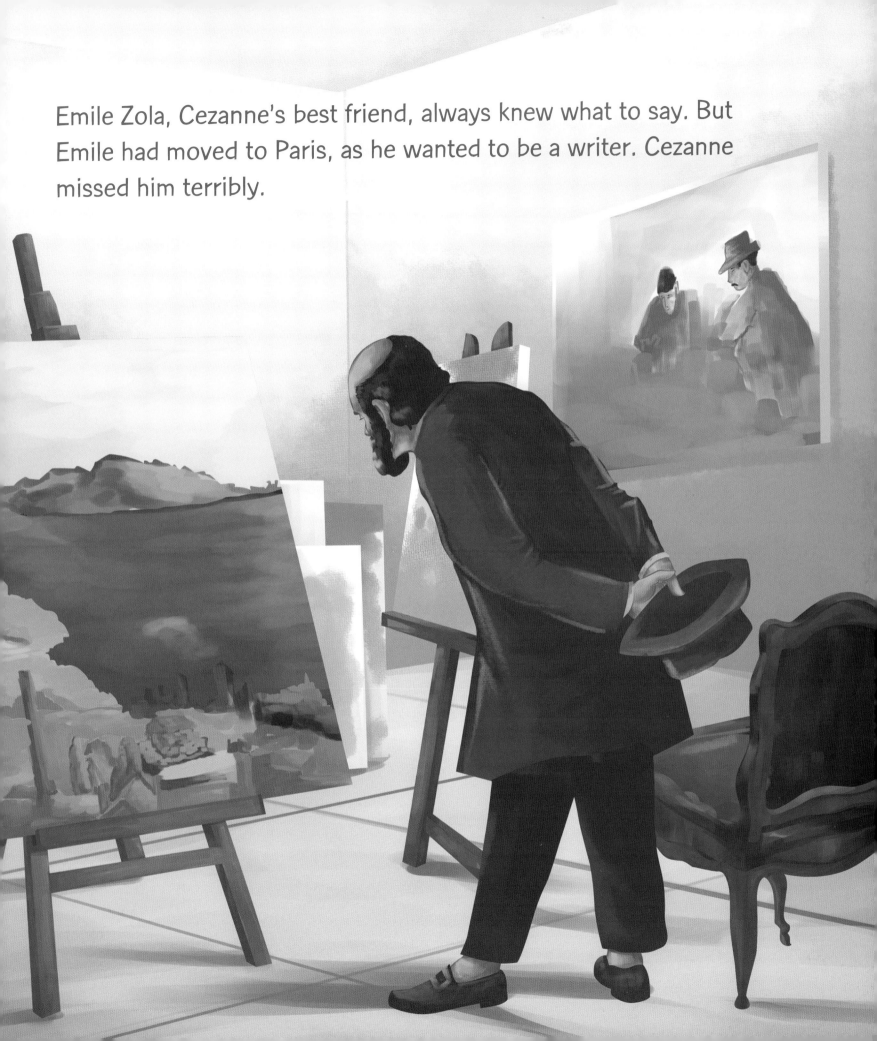

Emile Zola, Cezanne's best friend, always knew what to say. But Emile had moved to Paris, as he wanted to be a writer. Cezanne missed him terribly.

The next morning Cezanne set off to the countryside.

*What if I try something different?* thought Cezanne.

He set his canvas facing the beautiful rolling hills of Aix-en-Province. It was the painting of an apple that he had done earlier. He put a thick layer of paint on it and then took out a palette knife with which he scraped it off. He continued to alternate between scraping and slapping the paint. After nearly three hours, Cezanne stepped back to view the painting.

'Noooooo!' he screamed and tore the painting in a rage.

That evening a letter arrived from Emile. Cezanne put it away unread. He just could not bear to read it as he missed his friend dearly.

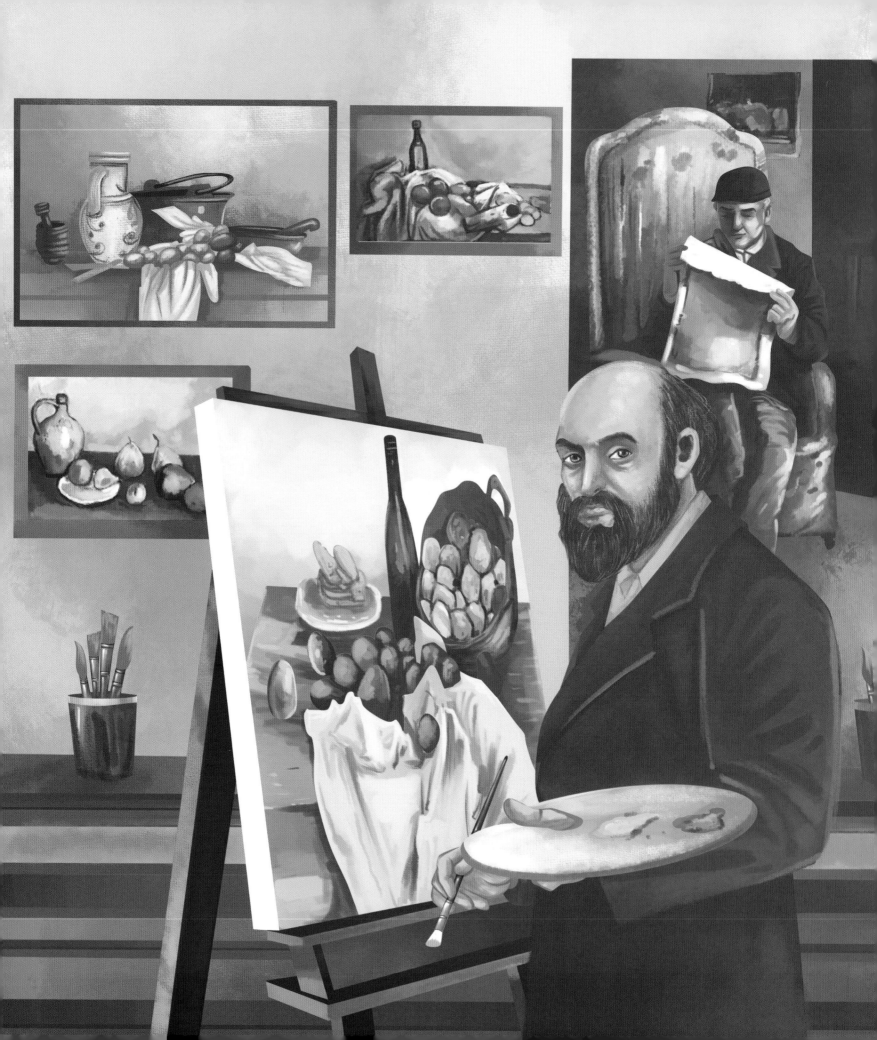

Each day Cezanne continued this routine with the painting of the apple.

'Son, why don't you come and work in the bank?' his father asked as usual.

Cezanne could see disappointment in his father's eyes. Not a single painting had sold.

*I will astonish Paris with an apple*! Cezanne thought, *How can I go and add numbers in a bank?*

He quickly packed his suitcase and slipped Emile's letter into his pocket. He would need his address in Paris.

'Remember son, we die with genius but we eat with money,' said his father to Cezanne as he left for Paris.

As Cezanne walked into Emile's apartment, he was surprised by the number of people in the tiny room.

There were fashionable ladies dressed in fur. Gentlemen in crisp suits smoked cigars and a musician played the upright piano in the corner of the room. Wine and champagne glasses were filled and emptied, just as quickly.

Cezanne checked the number of the apartment again. Yes, it was Emile's house.

'Cezanne, my dear friend,' shouted Emile, emerging from one of the back rooms.

But Cezanne could barely recognise his friend. He looked dapper in a suit but so different from the Emile he knew.

Cezanne barely heard the names of all the fancy people that Emile introduced him to. He felt awkward in his country suit.

The next morning Cezanne set off to the galleries to show his work. Perhaps someone in Paris would be interested.

'But Monsieur this is too bold,' said one of the dealers, staring at the painting.

By now Cezanne had perfected his technique of *couillarde* with a palette knife. Yet it was too bold for anyone to take a chance on it.

That evening Cezanne thought he could take it no longer.

He sat across Emile, 'Do you think I am a failure?'

'Not at all, Cezanne, you are a genius,' said Emile.

But Cezanne was not convinced.

'How can it be...no one, no one has bought a painting. They think I am a fool,' he shouted.

'Cezanne, Cezanne. My friend. They are the fools,' said Emile.

But somewhere Cezanne felt that Emile was also doubting him.

The next morning Cezanne caught the train to Aix.

Cezanne did not speak to anyone for days. He just painted and painted and painted.

Emile letters were left unopened. They slowly dwindled as Cezanne did not write back.

Many months later, Cezanne received a thick package in the mail. It was from Emile.

*What is this?* he thought.

He unwrapped it quickly to find a book and a letter from Emile.

'This is for you my friend, it is being received very well in Paris,' said the letter.

It was a copy of *L'Ouvre.*

Cezanne was excited. He had already read the first book by Emile about *Claude Lantier*, the protagonist of the book who is a painter.

Cezanne read the book from cover to cover all night. As the day broke, Cezanne reread the end. The book ended with Claude Lantier, the genius painter hanging himself in front of his painting.

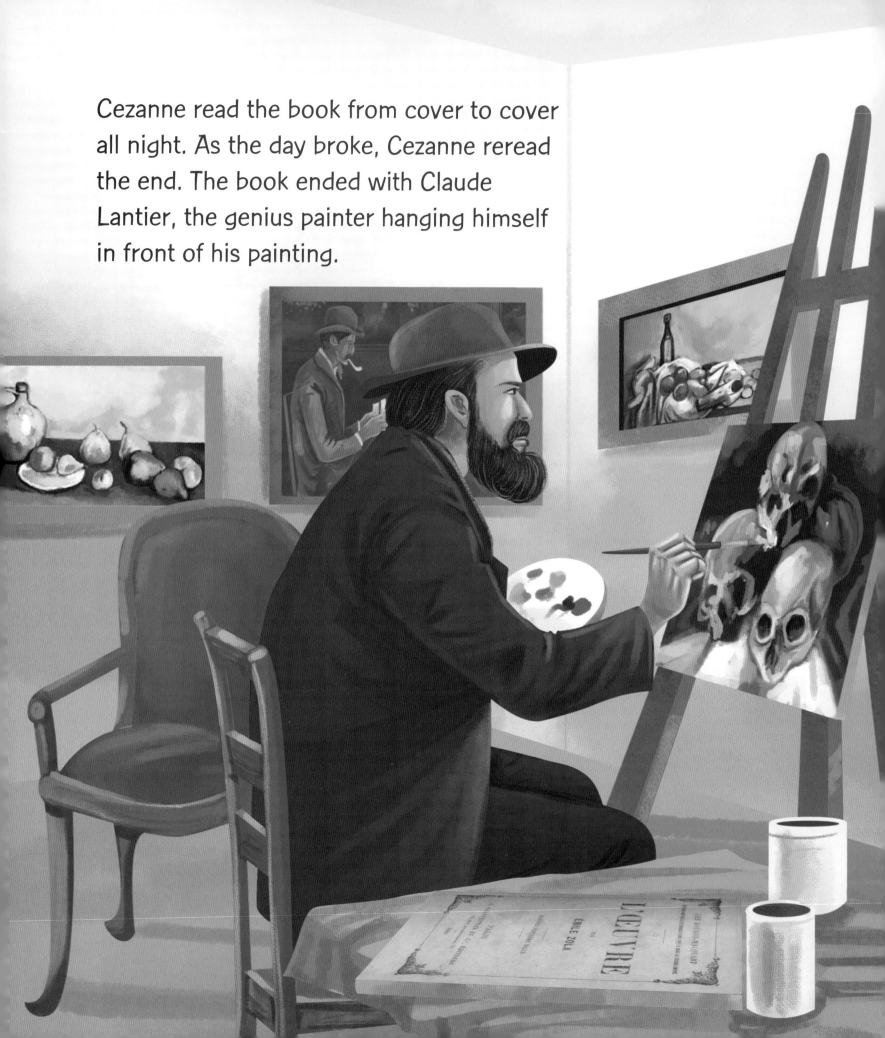

*Emile is this what you think of me?* thought Cezanne. Tears rolled down his cheek.
'Even you think I am a failure, Emile,' whispered Cezanne to no one in particular, 'We die with genius but we eat with bread.'

Paul Cezanne was born to a wealthy banker in 1839 in Aix-en-Provence, France.

Cezanne studied at the Free Drawing School.

His family forced him to attend law school but he dropped out of it and went to Paris to study art.

In Paris, he met Camille Pissarro who taught Cezanne the use of colour and encouraged him to study art.

In 1863, Cezanne had his first exhibition in the Salon Des Refuses, a salon that exhibited avant-garde artists who had been rejected by the prestigious Salon (Paris).

Cezanne married Hortense Fiquet, a French artist's model (1886) and had a son by her.

Cezanne is known to often stand for hours in the countryside and observe his subject, the countryside.

In 1906, Cezanne died due to exposure as he often painted in the rain, outdoors.